£1.00

The Covenant

BY DICK DAVIS

Dick Davis

The Covenant

Poems 1979 – 1983

Anvil Press Poetry

Published in 1984
by Anvil Press Poetry Ltd
69 King George Street London SE10 8PX
ISBN 0 85646 124 5

This book is published
with financial assistance from
The Arts Council of Great Britain

Photoset in Baskerville by
Katerprint Co Ltd, Oxford.
Printed in England at
The Arc & Throstle Press
Todmorden, Lancs.

FOR AFKHAM

Poems in this collection have previously been published in *Agenda*, *Helix*, *The Listener*, *Other Poetry*, *Poetry Review*, *PN Review* and *The Times Literary Supplement*. 'In the Gallery' appeared in the Mandeville Press pamphlet *Mandeville's Travellers*, 1984; 'The Jigsaw' was broadcast on BBC's *Poetry Now*. Nine poems were included in a pamphlet *Visitations*, Ampersand Press, 1983; the four 'Visitations' were also published as a chapbook by the Aralia Press, Westchester, Pa., 1984. Sixteen poems were published as *What the Mind Wants*, Robert L. Barth, Florence, Ky., 1984.

Contents

The Covenant

Fräulein X

And it turned out that with her thanks for the poison
Fräulein X had still one more request: would the friend
sing Brahms's 'Vier ernste Gesänge' before they parted.
DIARY OF RECK-MALLECZEWEN, DECEMBER 1938

Unseen, preserved beneath dark velvet, lie
Pale water-colours fugitive to light –
Displayed to none but friendship's gentler eye,
The sanctuaries of her sequestered sight –

Views of the Rhine and of the Holy Land,
Deep vistas of the spirit's need and rest:
Frail on glass shelves Venetian glasses stand,
The keepsakes of a life secure and blessed.

Now, in this last desire, she redeclares
Old faith in what is hers – Judaic psalms,
The German tongue: that heritage she shares
– Immutably – with Luther and with Brahms:

And though that sheltered world her childhood knew
Is shrunk to a dark room, though in the street
The mob bays hatred to the German Jew,
This covenant survives, beyond defeat.

In the Gallery

O patria mia!

One drawing held her; it was of
An indistinct but Eastern view
And had no special charm: her hand
Strayed to the glass as if she knew
The contours of that barren land
And could not stare at them enough:

I saw her beauty then, the love
Made steady in her exiled eyes:
Those lines were faint as memory,
Effaced as the elusive sighs
That scarcely broke her revery;
I watched, withheld, and could not move.

Portrait Painter

If, in the middle-aged
Worn face now given to
His stranger's scrutiny
He sees – unbidden, true –
Regret stare unassuaged
From posed formality –

Her need and loss, a life
Of compromise made plain,
His thoughts are not the rush
Of sympathy for pain
But tone and palette-knife,
The texture of this brush:

And, glancing up, his gaze
Meets nothing of the heart
But colour, shade, and gloss –
The problems of his art;
While from the canvas blaze
Discovered need and loss.

What the Mind Wants

Young aspens mirrored in a stream;
A guileless evanescence, an
Unguided turning to the wind.

But also the persistent weight
Of glassy water, the steady
Pressure that seems barely moving;

The windless, slow, reflective depth.

The Jigsaw

The portrait of the princess lies
In scattered fragments on the floor;
Crouched over them a young girl tries
Edges that would not fit before,

That sulk recalcitrant . . . ah there
Two pieces kiss: a greyish mass
That could be clouds or that patch where
Her dress half hides the shadowed grass.

The afternoon wears on: she sifts
And sorts; a piece is placed, withdrawn;
She sits up suddenly and lifts
Impatient arms. A stifled yawn.

And stoops again. Here no one wins,
It is a world you make and enter.
The edge is finished – now begins
The serious business of the centre.

A face emerges and young hands
Lie loose against grey silk; the eyes
Are guileless: almost there, she stands
Bent slightly forward in surprise.

Annunciation

Thin-shouldered, shy,
And much alone –
Anxious to screen
The monotone

Of her young life
From avid eyes,
The curious gaze
Disarmed by sighs,

By silence . . . but,
At heart, ashamed –
As if she knew
That she were blamed

For some dark sin
Unspecified –
As if the flesh
That broke her pride

Were penance for
An obscure fault
Not to be cleansed
In her tears' salt.

*

The morning lightens
Through poplar trees –
Her flushed skin takes
Dawn's sober breeze

As promise of
The known and real
To which she would
But cannot kneel.

And the light deepens
Beyond the line
Of glittering trees;
Their thin leaves shine

Till they are lost
In whelming light
Like water breaking . . .
She shields her sight

And hears the words
That justify
Her flesh, her life . . .
The unearthly cry

That battens on
Her faltering heart,
Naming her pure,
Elect, apart.

Four Visitations

Baucis and Philemon

Life lies to hand in hoe, spade, pruning-knife,
Plain wooden furniture and wattle walls,
In those unspoken words 'my husband', 'wife',
In one another's flesh which still recalls

Beneath the map of age their savoured youth.
It is an ambience in which they move
Having no need to grasp or grub for truth;
It is the still persistence of their love.

That one should die before the other's death
And drain the world of meaning is their fear:
Their hope, to draw together their last breath
And leave the sunlight on a common bier.

Life is the meaning and the bread they share;
Because they need no Gods, the Gods are there.

Semele

I imagine an English Semele –
A gawky girl who strayed beyond the town
Picking at stalks, alarmed by puberty . . .
Who by the handsome stranger's side lay down

And when he'd gone lay still in meadow-sweet
Knowing herself betrayed into the world –
Soft flesh suffused with summer's placid heat,
The clement light in which the ferns uncurled.

Both faded; meeting him again she sought
For that half-apprehended, longed-for power –
The glitter haunting her distracted thought
That seemed to peer from every leaf and flower,

The glory of the God . . . the girl became
The landscape's ghost, the sunlight's edgy flame.

Jacob I

This mother's darling, picksome in his pride,
Who lives by smiles, deceit, dumb-insolence,
Is sent out to secure a fitting bride
And takes the road in high self-confidence.

By noon there is no road – no shadows move
But his; the desert light glares hard and clear,
A lucid proof that he is owed no love,
That what pervades his solitude is fear.

The young man sleeps, his head propped on a stone,
Exposed to starlight and the vacant skies:
The angels climb, descend, and he is shown
Their ladder's length drawn up from where he lies.

First light, and cold air chills the dreamer's face
Waking to silence, in an empty place.

Jacob II

By sunset they had reached a shallow stream:
The women crossed and he was left alone
Unable to advance. As in a dream
A man with features known but scarcely known

Stood in his path and in the dusk they closed,
Strained sinew against sinew silently:
Who was the stranger whom his strength opposed,
The dark shape jealous of his liberty?

Dawn came, and locked within their stubborn fight
The traveller knew whose arms withheld him there;
'Bless me' he cried, 'Bless me before the light
Dissolves your substance to resistless air'

And one whom strength and skill could not confound
Was forced by benediction to the ground.

St Eustace

At dusk in the dark wood
The stag I'd harried stood –
Its wet flanks flecked with blood

The antlered head held high
As if not he but I
Were hunted here to die;

Between his tines the air
Grew solid to my stare;
The cross of Christ hung there –

I marked where he had bled;
Bright on his thorn-crowned head
The blood shone newly shed –

And as the moonlight broke
Through ash and smothering oak
The dead man moved and spoke.

Getting There

Now you approach the long prepared for place
The language you have learnt, the map you know
Seem childishly inadequate to show
Its obvious, unformulable grace.

But you were told that it would be like this
– An interim, an emptiness – a state
In which, like an expectant child, you wait
Not knowing what it is you must not miss.

Uxor Vivamus . . .

The first night that I slept with you
And slept, I dreamt (these lines are true):
Now newly-married we had moved
Into an unkempt house we loved –
The rooms were large, the floors of stone,
The garden gently overgrown
With sunflowers, phlox, and mignonette –
All as we would have wished and yet
There was a shabby something there
Tainting the mild and windless air.
Where did it lurk? Alarmed we saw
The walls about us held the flaw –
They were of plaster, like grey chalk,
Porous and dead: it seemed our talk,
Our glances, even love, would die
With such indifference standing by.
Then, scarcely thinking what I did,
I chipped the plaster and it slid
In easy pieces to the floor;
It crumbled cleanly, more and more
Fell unresistingly away –
And there, beneath that deadening grey,
A fresco stood revealed: sky-blue
Predominated, for the view
Was an ebullient country scene,
The crowning of some pageant queen
Whose dress shone blue, and over all
The summer sky filled half the wall.

And so it was in every room,
The plaster's undistinguished gloom
Gave way to dances, festivals,
Processions, muted pastorals –
And everywhere that spacious blue:
I woke, and lying next to you
Knew all that I had dreamt was true.

To His Wife

after Ausonius

Let us, dear wife, still live
As we have lived and keep
Those names we learnt to give
When we evaded sleep

On that first blessèd night.
O never dawn the day
When we forgo the rite
By which to you I say

'My girl' and you to me
'Young man'. Though we grow old
As ancient sages we
Shall not grow gravely cold:

Wisdom will be to know
The sweetness of the years –
Unnumbered they shall go,
Unwept for by our tears.

Travelling

You live for landscapes scudding past, the sense
That what sustains you is mere transience;

And for the dew immobile in each dawn –
The one clean stillness everywhere reborn.

Bath

for John and Joyce Jarvis

What draws us here is ordered elegance,
The spirit of a well-proportioned place,
As though the fading echoes of a dance
Still lingered and a girl in cotton lace

White broderie-anglaise and filmy lawn
Slipped from her chaperone to take the arm
Of an attentive beau and dance till dawn:
It is the cadence of a distant charm.

What drew the sick for centuries before
This architectural minuet began
Was that obscure, unending, chthonic roar –
The steamy cavern where the waters ran:

And from the airy Pump Room we go down
To sip the channelled dark beneath the town.

A Short History of Chess

When chess began in India
The bishops charged as elephants,
The queen was still a minister
And both were clearly combatants

In battles secular and male.
Who claims that Eastern ways perplex?
It took the West to twist the tale
To strategies of faith and sex.

Epigrams

ON EPIGRAMS

This neat, egregious house-style
Parades its insights pat, on time:
It smiles a very knowing smile . . .
Here comes another fucking rhyme.

(Its *double entendres* are subtle, supple –
'To fuck' here means, of course, 'to couple'.)

THE HOUSEHOLDER'S BONFIRE

Splashed paraffin: the avid first flame licks
From crumpled paper to the heaped dead sticks.

I step back to avoid the swirling sparks;
My neighbour comes and badgers me with Marx –

Das Kapital, the crumbling bourgeois state;
My garden's tidy now – I close the gate.

CRITIC TO POET

My scribbling summons you: you mount the stair
And stand, a mute admonishment, so near
I could not turn: my bent back knows your stare,
Each nuance of your mockery; your sneer.

THE MALADY OF THE QUOTIDIAN

We brood on money and forget to love.
The mild depression of the afternoon
Gives way to alcohol and Wagner's dove
Appeasing *Sehnsucht* on the gramophone.

OFF-SHORE CURRENT

Though I'd been warned I once
Ridiculously dived
Into that turbulence –
God knows how I survived.

I could not now repeat
Such glib insouciance
When caution bids retreat –
I didn't catch her glance.

A Letter to Omar

I stood beside the ghastly tomb they built for you
And shuddered with vicarious, mute guilt for you;
Are concrete columns what they thought you meant?
I wanted wine, a glass turned down, drops spilt for you.

A sick child reads (his life is not imperilled –
He sucks the candied death-wish of FitzGerald);
I was that child, and your translated words
Were poetry – the muse's gaudy herald.

Was it for you I answered that advertisement
Before I knew what coasting through one's thirties meant?
If so I owe my wife and child to that
Old itch to get at what your Englished verses meant.

Thus in your land I doled out Shakespeare, Milton –
Decided I preferred sheep's cheese to stilton
But knew as much of Persia or Iran
As jet-lagged fat cats sluicing at the Hilton.

My language-teacher was a patient Persian Jew
(I pray that he survives), a techno-person who
Thought faith and verse *vieux jeux*; he thought me weird –
He learnt my loyalties and his aversion grew.

Love proved the most effective learning lure and not
His coaxing tact: my girl required the score and plot
– Explained in halting, pidgin syllables –
Of our first opera (which was – aptly – *Turandot*).

When I had said, in crabbed words bare of ornament,
What *La Bohème*, *The Magic Flute* and *Norma* meant
She married me; my Persian was still bad
But now I knew I knew what 'nessun dorma' meant.

We set up home . . . but I feel more than sure you
Would nod assent to Dr Johnson's poor view
Of tulip streaks (*Damn all particulars . . .*)
And I desist – I wouldn't want to bore you.

2

You left the busy trivia unspoken:
Haunted by vacancy, you saw unbroken
Miles of moonlight – time and the desert edge
The high-walled gardens, man's minute, brief token.

And if I revelled in your melancholy
(Like mooching through the rain without a brolly)
It was the passion of your doubt I loved,
Your castigation of the bigot's folly.

Besides, what could be more perversely pleasant
To an ascetic, hungry adolescent
Than your insistent *carpe diem* cry
Of let conjecture go, embrace the present?

And all set out (I thought so then, I think so now)
In stanzas of such finely-wrought, distinct know-how
They were my touchstone of the art (it is
A taste our pretty *literati* think low-brow).

Such fierce uncertainty and such precision!
That fateful metre mated with a vision
Of such persuasive doubt . . . grandeur was your
Decisive statement of our indecision.

Dear poet-scholar, would-be alcoholic
(Well, is the wine – or is it not – symbolic?)
You would and would not recognize the place –
Succession now is quasi-apostolic,

The palace is a kind of Moslem Deanery,
But government, despite this shift of scenery,
Stays as embattled as it ever was –
As individual, and as sanguinary.

The warring creeds still rage – each knows it's wholly right
And welcomes ways to wage the martyrs' holy fight;
You might not know the names of some new sects
But, as of old, the nation is bled slowly white.

3

Listen: 'Death to the Yanks, out with their dollars!'
What revolution cares for poet-scholars?
What price evasive, private doubt beside
The public certainties of Ayatollahs?

And every faction would find you a traitor:
The country of the Rubaiyat's creator
Was fired like stubble as we packed our bags
And sought the province of its mild translator.

East Anglia! – where passionate agnostics
Can burn their strictly non-dogmatic joss-sticks,
And take time off from moody poetry
For letters, crosswords, long walks and acrostics;

Where mist and damp make most men non-committed,
Where both sides of most battles seem half-witted,
Where London is a world away and where
Even the gossips felt FitzGerald fitted;

He named his boat *The Scandal* (no misnomer . . .)
And fished the coast from Lowestoft round to Cromer,
One eye on his belovèd Posh, and one
On you or Virgil, Calderon or Homer;

Then wrote his canny, kind, retiring letters
To literature's aggressive, loud go-getters –
Carlyle and others I forbear to name
Who had the nerve to think themselves his betters;

You were the problems (metrical, semantic)
From which he made an anglicized Romantic –
The perfect correspondent for his pen
(Inward, mid-century, and not too frantic);

As you are mine in this; it makes me really sick
To hear men say they find you crass or merely slick;
Both you and your translator stay my heroes –
Agnostic blessings on you both!
                              Sincerely, Dick.

November 1982

Exiles

The two friends fill their time with chess: black plays
Decisively – white dithers and delays,

Picks up a pawn, stares, scowls, then puts it back;
He sees that his spectacular attack

Has turned into a tedious defence.
He cannot win but keeps up the pretence

Of caring how he loses and to whom.
The wives are chatting in another room;

Their rumours rise in disconnected scraps –
'and gold' – 'but X was shot' – 'the prince perhaps' –

'and she got out with nothing, so she says.'
White sees a move that prettily delays

Black's victory . . . 'my dear, that's just her joke.'
'No, no – she claims she's *absolutely* broke.'

Black pauses now and white turns round to shout
'Sweet, who are you two gossiping about?'

Woman on a Beach

How mild, how equable, are sun and sea.
The lean, lithe body of my child at play
Is not distinct from its desire, and I
Acknowledge, and inhabit, no desire.

Two East Anglian Poems

Trattando l'ombre come cosa salda
DANTE, PURGATORIO XXI.136

With John Constable

Slow-rotting planks and moody skies;
I look with your impassive eyes

Whose tact is love for what is there –
The worked soil and the moving air,

The reticence of grief: I hear
Through silence your dead voice draw near –

Those words you gave to Ruisdael's art,
'It haunts my mind, clings to my heart.'

Edward FitzGerald

East Anglia, a century ago:
    I see FitzGerald bow
    To Attar's *Conference*
        As I do now

Leaning through silence to a dead man's mind,
    A stranger's pilgrimage
    (As is the book we read)
        To a blank page –

An immanence, remote, but quickened by
    An old, ill scholar's breath:
    I see you wrest this life
        From brother death.

The Tribe of Ben

How easy now to mock
Those who wrote looking back
To rare Ben Jonson's line –
Firm royalists to a man

Unfitted for the claims
Of chiliastic times,
Preferring penury
To the trimmer's smooth way.

Filed epigram and lyric
Held Fanshawe, Lovelace, Herrick
From lazy shame; each sought
In his obscured retreat

Not rage or grief but grace,
An undeluded peace.
Hear how such passion gives
Perfected verse its voice.

A Photograph: Tehran, 1920s

How false, incongruous, each prop
That crowds into your photograph –
The stiff, fake flowers, the painted drop
To signal opulence (park-gates
Your shoulder half obliterates),
The draped and tasselled table-top

Against which you benignly lean.
A slight smile ghosts your bearded face
As you confront the strange machine
Which traps you in your mullah's robe
(A signal now that half the globe
Can snigger at and call obscene).

Your gaze holds mine: I know that you
Were never rich, depraved, or mad;
That at your death a rumour grew
Of unemphatic sanctity;
That your frail legend troubles me;
That all the signals are untrue.

Richard Davis

> . . . *minding to have sent to Qazvin Alexander Kitchin,*
> *whom God took to his mercy the 23rd October last: and*
> *before him departed Richard Davis one of your mariners . . .*
>
> HAKLUYT, PRINCIPAL VOYAGES
> OF THE ENGLISH NATION

Our mariner's last landfall was this shore:
My namesake stood, four hundred years ago,
The empty Caspian at his back, and saw
A shelving view I intimately know –

Clean, silent air and noble poplar trees,
A marshy plain beyond which mountains rise,
The snow-line and the sky – all this he sees –
The colours fresh and calm before his eyes.

Fresh as your fading figure in my mind:
You look back to your little ship, then stare
As if the riches you had hoped to find
Were somehow present in the limpid air.

You walk towards the limits of my sight –
I see you stumble in the dusty light.

On an Etching by J. S. Cotman

I wept to see the visionary man
DRYDEN'S VIRGIL

There is no richness in this scene,
No life to answer his abstracted stare –
And what we take it that these emblems mean
Is but the index of his inward care;

The summer-house will always stay
About to fall, the river make no sound
As Lethe-like it bears his strength away
And lapses to the darkness underground;

And poised above the silent flood
The couchant lion waits, a mask of stone,
Impassive by the tree that will not bud,
The spell-bound youth, beleaguered and alone.

The landscape is an open grave
At which the artist and his subject gaze;
When acid eats the plate, his skills engrave
Wanhope, a mind that falters and decays.

Early Morning, Salisbury Plain

Mist clinging to the contours of the land
And at my feet a roseate smear where ice
Reflects the late, low sun. I walk to lose
All sense of where I walk, but know barbed wire
And hawthorn line the path, swart branches spiked
Like wire through which the sun ascends and pales.
I pause and hear the intermittent boom
Of field-guns from the range.
                                    The mist will clear,
Is clearing now, particulars will claim
Rejection or allegiance from the heart.

Childhood of a Spy

Much earlier than most he found
Most things are not as they appear;
The mousy child who makes no sound
Lives in a haze of smothered fear –

Where is he safe? Reality
Is something glimpsed through misted glass;
A closed, adult conspiracy,
A frontier post he may not pass.

Truth is a secret and he learns
Its lonely code; the bit lip trembles
But says nothing – compassion turns
To hatred that a smile dissembles.

The frontier will be down, his fear
A state ubiquitous as air;
And, vindicated, he will hear
Their cry of candour and despair.

Near Coltishall

for Michael Riviere

Dark on the evening sky
(Though one gleams coldly bright
Caught by the sun's last light)
The thunderous aircraft fly
Into their deepening night:

Distracted from my page
I watch each passing plane –
The virtue of Montaigne
Is innocent to gauge
The wrath that they contain.

O privacy, retreat!
What fastness is secure
From that pervasive roar,
Who shall escape defeat
From what we dream of war?

(The village where I read
Is but a reference
On some chart marked 'Defence' –
Roofs overflown at speed
And of no consequence.)

Which would you choose, my lord –
The cant of government,
The smug cant of dissent?
Or would you turn toward
Your book's long argument

That wisdom is to know
How blindly we descend
To where no arms defend
Our ignorance from no
Imaginable end?

The Ransom

after Baudelaire

Man must, to pay his ransom, till
Two dark, rich fields through every season;
The blade that cuts the clay is Reason
Subservient to his patient will.

To make the least rose open there
Or wheat extend its meagre ears
He irrigates with grimy tears
The stubborn fields of his despair:

The one is Art, the other Love;
And when the law demands he pay
The ransom due on Judgement Day
Nothing will move the Judge above

But grain heaped in His granary,
And flowers whose loveliness is such
Their mingled forms and colours touch
The angels' hearts to clemency.

Mariam Darbandi

1956 – 1983

How frightened you were once
– And not so long ago –
When late one night we took
Our pathway homeward through
The churchyard where you saw
Grey gravestones row on row;

And afterwards we teased
Your childish, tense alarm
And mocked the way you clung
Against your sister's arm
As if you sensed the dead
Reach through the moonlit calm.

Dear child, I see you now,
Dear helpless fugitive –
To guide you past that place
What could I now not give?
The taint was in your blood
That would not let you live.

Earth holds you in her arms
And soothes you of your fear
And it is we who turn
To see the dead appear;
Who listen for the voice
We know we shall not hear.

Reading

The last page read you pat
With thoughtful tenderness
    Your novel's spine –
How much I'm moved by that
Improbable caress
    Which I thought mine.

I copied it from you?
You picked it up from me?
    Who knows which way
The gentle gesture flew . . .
It marks that privacy
    We both obey.

My Daughter Sleeping

Your eyelids are so thin
That as you sleep I see
The eyeballs dart within
That near transparency
Of blue-veined, restless skin.

What do you dream, my dear?
Already after less
Than five quick months your fear
Is fear at which I guess:
I kneel as if to hear

The whispered testament
Of what I cannot know –
My listening head is bent
To silence trapped below
That thin integument.

Auction – Job Lot

Framed, sepia photographs –
The blank eyes and the awkward pose,
Blurred faces no one living knows –
    These are their epitaphs.

Closed lives return our stare,
Heaped jumble in a cardboard box:
Curls in a locket that still locks,
    A Book of Common Prayer,

Its fly-leaf foxed and torn
Through the brief message and the date –
'To Meg., June Eighteen Fifty Eight,
    "In Christ we are reborn"',

Letters, a faded name,
Dried flowers . . . Value is of the heart,
The worth we cherish we impart
    And in our death reclaim.

A Christmas Poem

*Written for the 1982 Carol Service
of Nene College, Northampton*

One of the oxen said
'I know him, he is me – a beast
    Of burden, used, abused,
    Excluded from the feast –
    A toiler, one by whom
    No task will be refused:
I wish him strength, I give him room.'

One of the shepherds said
'I know him, he is me – a man
    Who wakes when others sleep,
    Whose watchful eyes will scan
    The drifted snow at night
    Alert for the lost sheep:
I give this lamb, I wish him sight.'

One of the wise men said
'I know him, he is me – a king
    On wisdom's pilgrimage,
    One Plato claimed would bring
    The world back to its old
    Unclouded golden age:
I wish him truth, I give him gold.'

Mary his mother said
'I know his heart's need, it is mine –
    The chosen child who lives
    Lost in his Lord's design,
    The self and symbol of
    The selfless life he gives:
I give him life, I wish him love.'

Two Love Songs

I

To love one who has loved
Is to be one who buys
A house whose tenant dies –
Whose ghost will not be moved.

Look – you are not alone;
The spectral revenant
Forestalls your steps to haunt
Places you call your own.

You have small cause to grieve:
When she confronts your eyes'
Cold, rancorous surmise
What ghosts does she perceive?

2

Kissing your hair
I glimpse your eyes –
Absent, elsewhere.
Who occupies
Your brooding stare

So that my kiss
Seems my illusion,
So that you miss
My brief confusion?
Come, answer this.

Who beckons you
Across what space,
Out of my view
In what blest place?
Who is it? Who?

Mute in my mind
The quarrel stays,
And unresigned
I watch your gaze –
Attentive, blind.

Abandoned Churchyards

The long grass covers
Untended graves –
Deep in its airy caves
Drowse summer lovers:

Flesh is subdued
To simple needs.
Think, where the rank grass seeds,
Love was pursued.

Hearing a Balkan Dance in England

The music gives itself, retreats:
Your mind's involuntary eye
Dazzles with fluttered handkerchiefs
Against a clear, Levantine sky;
In a quick pause the bride receives
Her groom's first kiss. The phrase repeats,

Repeats; again they dance.
                                          And you,
A stranger at the wedding-feast,
Caught up in happiness, were there
Until the circling rhythm ceased –
As now it ceases and the air
Of Norfolk's sky glows Iznik blue.

Translating Hafez

NORTH WEST FRONTIER, 1880s

for V. L. Clarke

I see the man I conjure – at a doorway
Bathed for a moment in the evening light
      And watching as the sun
      Descends behind bare hills

Whose shadow blurs, and renders substanceless,
Parade ground, barrack, flag-pole – the low step
      On which he stands; 'the hour
      Of cow-dust', but no herds

Are brought in here to shelter from the dark:
The bright, baroque commotion of the sky
      Is simplified to dusk
      In which the first stars shine

Like an admonishment that stills the heart.
He enters the dark house: though he is here
      By accident he makes
      His being of that chance,

Set down within a country which he loves
And which, he knows, cannot love him – so that
      His homage is a need
      Become its own reward

Unprized as that which Aristotle says
Souls nurture for the irresponsive God:
      A barefoot servant brings
      The oil-lamp and his books

(And in another dispensation he
Would be that grave, respectful, silent child).
      Moths circle him and tap
      The lamp's bright chimney-glass;

Now seated at his desk he opens text
And commentary; he dips his pen and writes
      'It is the night of power,
      The book of grief is closed . . .'

Exile

I turn from longing to the tasks life gives.
Beneath all surfaces your river flows –
I call you Grief. I shun you and I hear
Your murmur as I give myself to sleep.